Illinois

(Revised and Updated Edition)

by the Capstone Press
Geography Department

Content Consultant
Richard A. Capriola
Special Assistant to the Superintendent
Illinois State Board of Education

CAPSTONE BOOKS
an imprint of Capstone Press
Mankato, Minnesota

Capstone Books are published by Capstone Press
151 Good Counsel Drive, P.O. Box 669, Mankato, Minnesota 56002
http://www.capstone-press.com

Library of Congress Cataloging-in-Publication Data
Illinois/Capstone Geography Department.
        p. cm., -- (One nation)
    Includes bibliographical references (p. 46) and index.
    ISBN 1-56065-353-1
    1. Illinois--Juvenile literature. [1. Illinois.] I. Capstone
Press. Geography Dept. II. Series.
    F541.3.I45   1996
    977.3--dc20   95-49307
                                                    CIP
                                                    AC

Photo credits
Archive Photos, 22, 25, 26, 28
Daybreak Imagery, 30
Dept. of Commerce and Community, Illinois Bureau of
    Tourism, 4 (top)
Galena/Jo Daviess County Historical Society, 34
International Stock/Bobbe Wolf, 16, 18, 21
James P. Rowan, 10, 12
Visuals Unlimited, 39
Unicorn Stock/Russell R. Grundke, 4 (bottom); A. Gurmankin,
    5 (top); Ted Rose, 5 (bottom); B.W. Hoffmann, 6;
    Gurmankin/Morina, 9; Aneal Vohra, 32

Table of Contents

Fast Facts about Illinois

State Flag

Location:
Midwestern state in the north-central United States
Size: 56,400 square miles (146,640 square kilometers)

Population:
12,045,326 (1998 U.S. Census Bureau figures)
Capital:
Springfield
Date admitted to the Union:
December 3, 1818; the 21st state

Cardinal

Native Violet

Largest cities: Chicago, Rockford, Peoria, Springfield, Aurora, Naperville, Decatur, Elgin, Joliet, Evanston

Nicknames: Land of Lincoln, the Prairie State

State animal: White-tailed deer

State bird: Cardinal

State flower: Native violet

State tree: White oak

State song: "Illinois" by Charles H. Chamberlain and Archibald Johnston

White oak

5

Chapter 1

100 Stories Up

The elevator doors close. For a few seconds, the car is still. Then it begins to move. It zooms up.

Finally the car stops, and the doors open. The passengers walk out onto the Skydeck. They are on the 103rd floor of the Sears Tower in Chicago, Illinois. It is the second-tallest building in the world.

Skyscrapers

The first skyscraper was built in Chicago in the 1880s. Chicago architects began using steel

The Sears Tower in Chicago is the world's second-tallest building.

beams instead of stone to support their buildings.

Steel was necessary for skyscrapers. Buildings made only of stone could not be taller than about 10 stories. If a stone building is built any higher, it will collapse under its own weight.

Chicago now has three of the tallest office buildings in the world. The Sears Tower is 1,454 feet (436 meters) tall. The Amoco Standard Oil building is 1,136 feet (341 meters) tall. The John Hancock Center rises 1,127 feet (338 meters).

The Sears Tower was finished in 1973. It has 110 floors and more than 16,000 windows. From the top, a visitor can sometimes see Indiana to the southeast and Wisconsin to the north. Lake Michigan lies to the east.

From the Skydeck, a visitor can also see Chicago's busy airports, freeways, and railroads. Down below, cars and buses crowd the streets of the Loop. The Loop is the nickname for Chicago's downtown area. Chicago is the meeting point of the Midwest.

Chicago's downtown area is called the Loop.

Chapter 2

The Land

Illinois is a Midwestern state. It covers an area of 56,400 square miles (146,640 square kilometers). The Mississippi River flows along the western border. Lake Michigan is at the northeast corner. Farms take up more than 80 percent of the land in Illinois.

Most of Illinois is flat. It is called the Prairie State because 60 percent of Illinois is prairie. Thirty percent of the land is hills with prairie and 10 percent is hills. The main hill areas are the Shawnee Hills in the south, the Lincoln Hills in the west, and the Dubuque Hills in the northwest.

Farms take up more than 80 percent of the land in Illinois.

Northern Illinois

   Steep hills rise between the rivers of the northwest corner. Rocky bluffs line the streams. In Jo Daviess County, Charles Mound reaches 1,235 feet (376 meters). It is the highest natural point in Illinois. Starved Rock State Park is also located in northern Illinois.

Visitors climb a frozen waterfall at Starved Rock State Park.

In the northeast, Chicago sprawls along the shores of Lake Michigan. Canals link Lake Michigan with the Mississippi River.

The Central Plains

The Central Plains region covers most of Illinois. Farmers plow the fertile soil of the prairies. Fields of corn and other crops stretch for many miles.

The Shawnee Hills

The Shawnee National Forest crosses the Shawnee Hills in southern Illinois. There are steep hills, ravines, and waterfalls in the region. The Garden of the Gods is a valley with many strange rock formations.

The Ohio River flows along the southern border of Illinois. Caves formed in the hills in the Ohio Valley. River pirates once used these caves as hideouts.

Southern Illinois

At the southern tip of Illinois the land is mostly level. Wetlands border the Ohio and Mississippi rivers.

Cairo is the southernmost town in Illinois. Early settlers thought this part of Illinois looked like Egypt. They named the town after Cairo, the capital of Egypt.

Wildlife

Foxes, beaver, rabbits, squirrels, and raccoons live throughout Illinois. Wild ducks nest in the Illinois River Valley. Pheasants and quail fly over Illinois. Bass, catfish, and bluegills swim in the state's rivers and lakes.

Illinois Weather

The northern and southern parts of Illinois have different weather. The northern half of the state has cold winters and warm summers. The southern half has mild winters and hot summers.

In the spring and early summer, violent storms cross the plains of Illinois. The worst

tornado in history hit Illinois on March 18, 1925. The tornado crossed 200 miles (320 kilometers) at a speed of 62 miles (99 kilometers) per hour. The storm killed 695 people in Missouri, Illinois, and Indiana.

Chapter 3

The People

Illinois is the most populous Midwestern state. It is home to Polish Americans, African Americans, Greek Americans, Italian Americans, Asian Americans, Hispanics, and others. Many different languages can be heard on the streets of Chicago. Even some small towns have ethnic neighborhoods. About 80 percent of the population of Illinois is white.

Coming to Illinois

In the early 19th century, farmers came to Illinois from the eastern United States. They settled on homesteads and worked the state's fertile soil. Later, many immigrants came to the

There are Asian-American businesses in many Chicago neighborhoods.

Chicago's South Side is one of the largest African-American neighborhoods in the country.

cities of Illinois. They were looking for work in busy factories.

Europeans

European immigrants settled in the state. Many Illinois residents have German, Italian, or British ancestors. Chicago has large populations of ethnic Poles, Ukrainians,

Czechs, and Slovaks. For more than 100 years, eastern Europeans have made up a large part of the city's work force.

The first Europeans to settle in Illinois were French. Most came when Chicago was growing as an industrial center.

African Americans

African Americans make up about 15 percent of the Illinois population. About half the people of Chicago are African American.

Early in this century, many African Americans from the southern states moved to Chicago's South Side. This is still one of the largest African-American neighborhoods in the country.

Asian Americans

Illinois communities of Asian Americans grew after World War II and after the Vietnam War. There are Chinese, Vietnamese, Korean, and Thai stores in many Chicago neighborhoods.

Hispanics

Mexican Americans make up the largest part of the state's Hispanic population. Hispanics speak Spanish or have Spanish-speaking ancestors. There are also immigrants from Puerto Rico, Cuba, and Venezuela. Hispanics make up about 8 percent of the population. It is the fastest-growing ethnic group in the state.

Chicago's Ethnic Neighborhoods

Ethnic groups have their own large neighborhoods in Chicago. Many of the city's stores and restaurants have signs written in foreign languages. Halsted Street runs 20 miles through the middle of Chicago. Greektown and many other ethnic neighborhoods are along this street.

In the past, many Swedish immigrants moved to the Clark Street area on Chicago's North Side. They called the neighborhood Andersonville.

Hispanics make up about 8 percent of the state's population.

Chapter 4

Illinois History

The first people to live in Illinois were Native-American hunters. They called the land Illiniwek. It meant "the men." Later, the French changed the name to Illinois.

The French Arrive

Two Frenchmen, fur trader Louis Jolliet and Father Jacques Marquette, were the first Europeans in Illinois. They arrived by canoe in 1673. Marquette built a mission for the Kaskaskia Indians. In 1703, other priests founded the town of Kaskaskia. It was the first settlement in Illinois.

In the late 17th century, René Robert Cavelier, Sieur de La Salle, claimed the Illinois area for France.

In the late 17th century, René Robert Cavelier, Sieur de La Salle, claimed the Illinois area for France. But France lost Illinois and most of North America to England in the French and Indian War (1754-1763).

Revolutionary War

During the Revolutionary War (1775-1783), a frontiersman named George Rogers Clark raided English forts in Illinois. Clark's followers called themselves the Big Knives. They made Illinois a part of Virginia.

After the founding of the United States, settlers began coming to what is now Illinois. They came from Virginia, Kentucky, and Maryland. Illinois became a U.S. territory in 1809.

Indian Wars

Illinois became a state on December 3, 1818. Settlers from the east arrived and thousands of European immigrants poured into the state. The rush of people forced many Indians to move west across the Mississippi River.

George Rogers Clark, left, and his men raided British forts in Illinois during the Revolutionary War.

A chief named Black Hawk would not leave. In 1832, he led a band of 400 warriors against the settlers. The state organized militias for defense. The Black Hawk War ended with Black Hawk's defeat.

Abraham Lincoln

In 1858, Abraham Lincoln ran for the U.S. Senate against Stephen A. Douglas. The two men held a series of debates throughout Illinois. Lincoln lost the election but his stand against slavery, which was still allowed in the South, won national attention.

In 1860, Lincoln was elected president. Many Southern states left the Union. Lincoln did not want the United States to be split in

The Great Chicago Fire destroyed Chicago in 1871.

half. In April 1861, the Civil War broke out between the North and the South.

During the war, 250,000 troops from Illinois fought for the Union. Ulysses S. Grant, who led the Union forces, was from Illinois. The Union won the war in 1865. Lincoln was shot and killed by John Wilkes Booth five days after the South surrendered.

The Great Chicago Fire

By the end of the war, Chicago was the site of factories, meat-packing plants, and large neighborhoods. Then, disaster hit the city. On October 8, 1871, a fire destroyed 17,000 buildings and killed 300 people. The Great Chicago Fire burned for 31 hours. The city was destroyed.

Skilled architects helped rebuild the city. In 1885, the Home Insurance Building was completed. This was the world's first skyscraper.

Gangsters lined up during a 1940 police roundup in Chicago.

By the turn of the century, Chicago was the second-largest city in the United States. Only New York was larger.

Gangland Chicago

In the 1920s, the government passed laws that banned the sale of liquor. This was called Prohibition. During Prohibition (1920-1933), Chicago gangsters sold illegal beer and whiskey. The gangs fought with each other. There were many killings and shootouts.

The Great Depression (1929-1939) slowed Illinois' growth. Many workers lost their jobs. Many families lost their homes.

The economy began to recover in the late 1930s. There was new construction in the cities. An oil boom in southern Illinois provided many workers with jobs.

World War II and After

Hundreds of factories in Illinois produced arms, aircraft, and ammunition during World War II (1939-1945). The work brought the state out of the Great Depression. After the war, new and old industries helped Illinois to prosper.

In 1992, Illinois made political history. Its citizens elected Carol Moseley Braun as the first black woman to serve in the U.S. Senate.

In 1997, the Chicago Bulls basketball team made sports history. The Bulls won their fifth National Basketball Association championship in seven years.

Chapter 5

Illinois Business

Illinois began as a farming state. But manufacturing soon became an important part of the state's economy. Today, many people work in service industries. These include banks, insurance companies, hotels, restaurants, and many other businesses.

Agriculture

Farms take up more than 80 percent of the land in Illinois. Farmers grow soybeans, corn, wheat, and vegetables. They raise sheep, hogs, and dairy cattle.

Agriculture is still an important business in Illinois.

O'Hare International Airport serves about 190,000 passengers per day.

Manufacturing

There are nearly 20,000 factories in Illinois. These plants make steel, automobiles, farm equipment, paper, tires, transportation equipment, and hundreds of other items. Peoria is the home of the Caterpillar company. Tractors and heavy equipment are made there.

Communications

Chicago is a major communications and publishing center. It is the home of Johnson Publishing Company. It is the largest African American-owned publishing company in the world. Johnson publishes magazines like *Ebony, Jet,* and *EM.*

Mining and Energy

Illinois has more coal than any other state except Montana. But most of the coal is bituminous, or soft coal. Bituminous coal pollutes the air. Some cities do not allow their power plants to burn it.

Illinois also has lead, zinc, natural gas, and gravel. Illinois silica sand is used to make glass. The state produces much of its energy from 13 nuclear plants. That is more than in any other state.

Transportation and Tourism

People from all over the world travel through Chicago. O'Hare International Airport serves about 190,000 passengers a day.

Tourism is a big industry in Illinois, especially in Chicago. The Art Institute, the Museum of Science and Industry, and the Du Sable Museum of African-American History are all in Chicago.

Chapter 6

Seeing the Sights

Chicago attracts many visitors with its restaurants, nightclubs, and museums. But there are many other things to see in Illinois.

There are small towns that have changed little in 100 years. Old French and British forts have been rebuilt. For campers and hikers, there are parks and trails to explore.

Northern Illinois

The northwestern corner of Illinois includes the Dubuque Hills. The home of President Ulysses S. Grant still stands in Galena.

Hikers visit the Upper Mississippi Wildlife and Fish Refuge. The refuge protects birds, fish, and animals living in the Mississippi Valley. The Mississippi Palisades State Park

The home of President U.S. Grant still stands in Galena.

has steep cliffs and strange rock formations.

Starved Rock State Park is in La Salle County. According to a legend, a group of Illinois Indians fought a series of battles in the area. They were finally surrounded on top of a tall rock. Instead of surrendering, they starved themselves to death.

The city of Rockford lies along the Rock River. The river winds through northwestern Illinois and empties into the Mississippi. The main attraction in Rockford is the Time Museum. It has a collection of 3,000 kinds of clocks and timepieces dating back to the 1500s.

Chicago

In the northeastern corner of Illinois, Chicago and its suburbs sprawl along the shore of Lake Michigan.

Visitors can view exhibits of reptiles, invertebrates, and thousands of varieties of sea life at the Shedd Aquarium. The Field Museum of Natural History displays towering dinosaur skeletons.

Brookfield and Oak Park are two suburbs of Chicago. The Brookfield Zoo has more than 2,800 animals. Oak Park is one of Chicago's oldest suburbs. It is home to many buildings designed by famous architect Frank Lloyd Wright.

Saganaki, a Greek dish of flaming cheese, started in Chicago. Deep-dish pizza, also known as Chicago-style pizza, also started there.

Every summer, the city holds the Taste of Chicago festival. Visitors can sample hundreds of different ethnic foods. Rock and jazz bands play in Grant Park.

Central Illinois

Huge fields of crops cover the plains of central Illinois. Peoria is the largest city in the region. Southwest of Peoria is Dickson Mounds State Park. It is an ancient Indian burial ground. Prehistoric pottery and tools are on display.

Abraham Lincoln's home is in Springfield, the state capital. Northwest of Springfield is New Salem State Park. Lincoln lived in New Salem as a young man. The town has been rebuilt to look as it did when Lincoln lived there.

The University of Illinois is in the twin cities of Champaign and Urbana. The university has more than 34,000 students.

Douglas and Moultrie counties have many Amish farmers. The Amish are very religious.

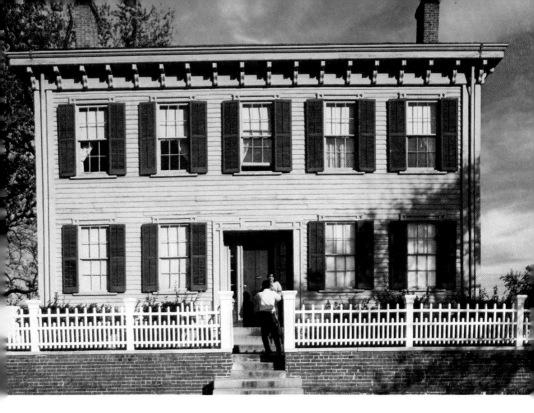

Abraham Lincoln's former home is located in Springfield.

They live much as their ancestors did. They use horse-drawn plows. They do not use cars or electricity.

Darwin is on the Indiana border. A ferryboat there carries cars across the Wabash River, which separates Indiana and Illinois.

Southern Illinois

Southern Illinois is mostly farmland. There are no big cities. Some people make their living by mining coal or drilling for oil.

The state's largest forests are in the Shawnee National Forest, which crosses southern Illinois. The Garden of the Gods is named for towers and cliffs of rock that rise from the hills.

Dixon Springs State Park is on the site of an early Illinois settlement. There are river canyons and waterfalls. At one time, people came to a health spa that was built on the site of a mineral spring.

The ancestors of many who live in southern Illinois came from southern states. You can still hear southern accents in some small towns.

Illinois Time Line

About 8000 B.C.—Early people are living in Illinois.

800s—Native Americans build huge earthen mounds as sites for temples and burials.

1500s—Several Native American groups form the Illiniwek Confederation.

1673—French explorers become the first Europeans to visit Illinois.

1763—British troops take control of Illinois.

1779—A Haitian named Jean Baptiste Point du Sable builds a trading post on the site of present-day Chicago.

1818—Illinois becomes the 21st state.

1832—The Sauk and Fox people are driven from Illinois during the Black Hawk War.

1837—John Deere builds the first steel plow in Grand Detour, Illinois.

1865—President Abraham Lincoln is assassinated in Washington, D.C., and is buried in Springfield, Illinois.

1871—The Great Chicago Fire destroys much of the city.

1885—The Home Insurance Building in Chicago becomes the world's first modern skyscraper.

1900—The Chicago Sanitary and Ship Canal is completed.

1929—Al Capone's orders to kill members of "Bugs" Moran's gang result in the St. Valentine's Day Massacre.

1959—The opening of the St. Lawrence Seaway allows oceangoing ships to reach Chicago.

1968—Protests against the Vietnam War disrupt the Democratic National Convention in Chicago.

1981—Ronald Reagan, who was born in Tampico, becomes the 40th U.S. president.

1997—The Chicago Bulls win their fifth NBA championship in seven years.

Famous Illinoisans

Jane Addams (1860-1935) Social worker who founded Hull House (1889) for Chicago's poor and immigrants; born in Cedarville.

Black Hawk (1767-1838) Sauk leader who fought in the War of 1812 and the Black Hawk War; born near Rock Island.

Carol Moseley Braun (1947-) Politician who became the first African-American woman in the U.S. Senate (1992); born in Chicago.

Hillary Rodham Clinton (1947-) Lawyer and activist who served as First Lady for her husband President Bill Clinton (1993-); born in Chicago.

Richard J. Daley (1902-1976) Politician who controlled Chicago's government as mayor from 1955 until his death; born in Chicago.

Miles Davis (1926-1991) Trumpet player who helped create "cool" jazz; born in Alton.

Walt Disney (1901-1966) Cartoonist and businessperson who created Mickey Mouse and built Disneyland; born in Chicago.

George Ferris (1859-1896) Inventor of the Ferris wheel; born in Galesburg.

Ernest Hemingway (1899-1961) Author who won the Nobel Prize (1954); his works include *The Old Man and the Sea*; born in Oak Park.

Wild Bill Hickok (1837-1876) Western scout and U.S. marshal; born in Troy Grove.

Jackie Joyner-Kersee (1962-) Track and field star who won gold medals at the 1988 and 1992 Olympic Games; born in East St. Louis.

Ronald Wilson Reagan (1911-) Actor and politician who served as 40th president of the United States (1981-1989); born in Tampico.

Carl Sandburg (1878-1967) Author and poet who won the Pulitzer Prize in history (1940) for *Abraham Lincoln: The War Years*; born in Galesburg.

Robin Williams (1952-) Actor who starred in *Mrs. Doubtfire, Toys, Jack,* and many other movies; born in Chicago.

Words to Know

debate—discussion of both sides of an issue

ethnic—a group with a common culture

Great Depression—period from 1929 to 1939 marked by unemployment, poverty, and hardship

immigrants—people who come to another country to settle

militia—citizens who are not professional soldiers called to serve in the armed forces during emergencies

mission—headquarters of people sent to do religious or charitable work in a territory or foreign country

prairie—large area of level or slightly rolling grasslands

Prohibition—a period from 1920 to 1933 when the U.S. government banned the manufacture and sale of alcoholic beverages

To Learn More

Brill, Marlene Targ. *Illinois.* Celebrate the States. New York: Benchmark Books, 1997.

McAuliffe, Emily. *Illinois Facts and Symbols.* Mankato, Minn.: Hilltop Books, 1998.

Santella, Andrew and Richard Conrad Stein. *Illinois.* New York: Children's Press, 1998.

Thompson, Kathleen. *Illinois.* Austin, Texas: Raintree Steck-Vaughn, 1996.

Internet Sites

City.Net Illinois
http://www.city.net/countries/united_states/illinois
Illinois Bureau of Tourism
http://www.enjoyillinois.com/
State of Illinois
http://www.state.il.us/
Travel.org-Illinois
http://travel.org/illinois.html

Useful Addresses

John Deere Historic Site
8393 South Main
Grand Detour
Dixon, IL 61021

Dickson Mounds State Museum
10956 North Dickson Mounds Drive
Lewiston, IL 61542

Illinois Bureau of Tourism
310 South Michigan Avenue
Chicago, IL 60601

John G. Shedd Aquarium
1200 South Lake Shore Drive
Chicago, IL 60605

Index